Retirement Strategies for the New Economy

Retirement Strategies for the New Economy

A Definitive Guide for Retiring Well

A Compilation of Financial Industry Thought Leaders

LEON SMITH
PUBLISHING

ISBN: 978-1-945446-86-3

This book is dedicated to the hardworking American men and women who sacrifice throughout their lives to save money for that proverbial rainy day called retirement.

Contents

Acknowledgments

First, we acknowledge the Lord for granting us the insight to develop this project.

We acknowledge the MEG team, especially our publishing consultant, Joe Feldkamp, without whose help this book would not be possible.

Lastly, we acknowledge the authors of this book, who work tirelessly to help their clients achieve their retirement goals and attain financial success.

Introduction

MEG has worked with our clients for many years to understand their branding and marketing goals. Over the years, each client has shared many stories about the various ways in which they help families prepare for retirement and ultimately retire well. These stories were the impetus for MEG to work with the authors of this book to share how they work with clients to help them reach their goals.

We recommend the readers of this book use it as a reference tool to garner ideas that can be applied to their investment strategies.

Whether you choose to work with a financial advisor to plan for the future or you choose to handle your own retirement planning, you can use the ideas in this book to help you:

- Create a top-ten list of ideas to apply to your future.
- Use the list to make smart investment decisions.
- Bring the list to a meeting with your advisor.
- Engage the advisor who gave you this book to answer all your questions and to help you create the best possible plan for your retirement.

The adjustments you make by using your list of investment strategies can make a really big difference. One small change can help you enjoy the retirement of your dreams. Use the ideas in this book to get you where you want to go.

Many pre-retirees and retirees worry about their money. You may find yourself asking questions like:

- *Will I have enough money to maintain my lifestyle during retirement?*
- *How will I handle unanticipated issues that occur like health care costs or helping to pay for my grandkids' college educations?*
- *Can I afford to travel to see my family around the country?*
- *Will my investments allow me to actively participate in my children's lives?*
- *Will my spouse and I be able to do all the things on our bucket list?*

Create peace of mind in your golden years by utilizing the wisdom contained in this book.

~ Mark Edward Gaffney

Develop a Retirement Plan for Greater Success

by Spencer Childs

I have been in this business since 1988. That's thirty-three years of experience. In all that time, I've learned that, for most people, the highest cost in investing is the emotional cost. We know that, in the long term, the stock market has appreciated. We have accurate records for the stock market reaching back to 1928. It is the best investment in the history of humankind that we have. The stock market, as a proxy for the U.S. economy, has provided exponential growth at an unbelievable rate.

I frequently ask my clients, "Why does the stock market go up?" or "Why does the stock market go down?"

I hear a lot of interesting answers to that question. Let me be specific: Stocks go up because there are more buyers than sellers. Stocks go down because there are more sellers than buyers.

So what's the problem?

When we buy stock, we try to buy low and sell high.

But if we buy low, what is everybody else doing?

They are selling.

If we sell when the stock market is high, what is everybody doing?

They are buying.

It is difficult to go against the emotional energy of the crowd. We are bombarded with nonstop information from social media, websites, and TV programs, like CNBC and Fox Business. We can become inundated with financial information, and it can freak us out. The important thing is to have a plan in place for your retirement, so you can sleep peacefully at night.

I live in Las Vegas, and I hear from professional gamblers and recreational gamblers all the time.

They come into a social setting and say: *I just won a big jackpot.*

Well, I have been in town long enough to know that if they've just won a big jackpot, that means they have lost at least four times as much as they have won in the last month. It's a stunning number. Feeling confident in a financial plan, no matter what happens with the marketplace, brings tremendous peace of mind. I like knowing that my family and I are taken care of. That's what is important to me.

My philosophy of financial planning is to keep everything on an even keel. Many people board an emotional roller coaster and react to what they hear from friends on social media or the news. They get scared and they sell. They sell right when they should be buying more because everybody is selling.

There is little barrier to entry into the stock market and little barrier to exit. When we are emotionally triggered, it is easy for us to react, and we can make decisions that are not in our best interest. The key for sleeping peacefully is to have a plan in place that persistently and consistently has proven to work in every economic climate. That is the goal.

Spend Less Than You Earn

This is a common question that I am asked:

What piece of advice is applicable to me or my family or somebody I love and care about?

The answer is not sexy or exciting; it is simple: spend less than you earn.

I can help you if you spend less than you earn. I cannot help you if you spend more than you earn. It does not matter what your income is. And it does not matter if you make a million dollars a month; I still cannot help you. It seems this *spending less than you earn* makes so much sense—is so common and unexciting—people simply ignore it.

Here are two examples: One of my clients, a physician, made between $50,000 and $80,000 a month—a month! He and his wife came from abject poverty, and I mean, real poverty, as far as the United States knows poverty. As a matter of fact, he is in his mid-sixties now, and he grew up in the United States without running water. They did not have indoor plumbing where he was raised in North Carolina. When he started making real money, his wife and he did not think that they could possibly spend it all. They were wrong. This physician, making $50,000 a month, had to borrow $10,000 dollars just to make his basic bills, and that is a stunning feature.

Another client who passed away five or six years ago—bless his heart—was a custodian at an elementary school in Las Vegas for fifty-three years. I managed $1.8 million for him, and he never made more than $45,000 a year. But the key is that he never spent more than $20,000.

The key to becoming financially independent or self-reliant in the United States is to spend less than you earn. If you can do that, then all your financial dreams can come true. If you cannot do that, nobody can help you.

Wants Versus Needs

The theme of this chapter is *Wants Versus Needs*, or how you bring into reality the concept that you *Spend Less Than You Earn*. For example, most of us need a car, and that car can run from $2,000 to $200,000. Most of us have a much nicer car than we *need*, but it is what we *want*.

Wants are not bad, but if we don't impose self-control on our wants, they eventually grow so great, there is no possible way of meeting them. The wants can cascade out of control. For example, the physician I referenced earlier started spending money on things like custom clothing. When I reviewed their checkbook and went on some basic ledger with them, we discovered they were spending an average of $22,000 a month on clothes. I pointed out to them that $22,000 means they'd have to make $45,000 pre-tax just to buy their clothes for the month.

If you had asked the physician's wife when he started medical school whether she'd be happy doing her shopping at JCPenney, she would have said yes. When he got out of medical school and was in residency, shopping at Nordstrom for her was great—more expensive, but great. But then, once he became a full-fledged doctor—heaven forbid she should go to a gala and meet another woman in the exact same dress. So now she has all her clothes custom made, all paid for using his salary.

Wants are also an expression and an extension of the ego. Especially now that we engage in the damaging effects of comparing ourselves to others on social media, we develop a competitive mindset: *My happiness or sadness is based on how much money I make or do not make, or judged by how much money I make compared to others.*

It's foolish to compare ourselves to others this way. It takes the power for my happiness out of my hands and puts it into the hands of others. Again, that is a game you cannot win. It can create real problems. You must control your emotions. You must control your wants versus your needs.

I approach investing in a holistic way, a way in which you create stable plans that save you from emotional extremes. We make poor decisions when we are driven by emotional extremes.

Controlling Our Egos

Controlling our egos is really another way of saying *controlling our emotions*. Focus on your goal, which for most of my clients is not to outlive their money. But here is the thing: Most of us have experienced economic problems, particularly when we were young. And those young experiences continue to inform our decision making as adults, whether or not we recognize it.

As we grow older, hopefully our situations improve. But some of my clients have a hard time comprehending what it is like to be eighty and have investment problems, as compared with being sixty or fifty or even seventy and having problems with their investments. Those are two totally different experiences.

So here is my point: if you are at retirement age or approaching retirement age, the game can be won if your choices remain conservative and bland.

The only thing we need to do is safely beat inflation and taxes, which is absolutely achievable. But it takes persistent and consistent effort, and you need to pull your ego out of it. You are never going to be at the country club or golf course with the guys and say, "I bought Microsoft at ten dollars a share," or, "I bought Apple computer before Steve Jobs came back." It's true that staying conservative means you're never going to have these huge victories.

But what you'll also never have, besides these victories, is you will never be hurt by a major problem in the economy. And here is the good news: The U.S. economy is the greatest economic engine in recorded history. I do not anticipate anything derailing it. Considering what we have already lived through as a nation—the Great Depression, WWII, the Cold War, the Cuban Missile Crisis, Vietnam, gas shortages in the seventies, double-digit interest rates—we can survive many setbacks. My dad bought a house in 1980 with 20 percent interest for the mortgage. The economy has persevered.

As a retiree on a sensible fiscal investment plan, you won't experience blowout years where you do really well, nor will you be hurt and do really poorly. If we pull our egos out, then we are not worried about the comparisons; we just need to beat inflation and taxes. If you can do that, it does not matter if you live to be 130; you are not going to run out of money.

If we do not plan well and sensibly—if we put ourselves in positions where we lose money, we go backward—then we can be an eighty-year-old with financial problems. And none of us wants to be in that position.

Understanding Interest

When I was teenager, my dad was trying to teach me something, and—God rest his soul—I wished I had listened better back then. He said, "Son, there are two types of people: those who understand interest and those that pay it. Think about that."

That is profound. Because if you understand interest, you will not pay it.

If you earn 5 percent interest on $10,000 over twenty-five years, it will grow to about $80,000. Now, instead of earning 5 percent, let's increase that to 10 percent. Your earning does not double. It goes up almost *six-fold*. Ten thousand dollars earning 10 percent over twenty-five years is going to be worth about $650,000. Again, same $10,000, same twenty-five years.

What if you could earn 20 percent interest?

In twenty-five years, you'd have in excess of $20 million. Interest grows exponentially, whether you're earning it or paying your creditors. So do not be fooled; you do not get ahead by borrowing money.

I learned another lesson from my dad when I overheard him telling my uncle, "Barry, you will never get out debt by borrowing money." It is so sad, it's funny. But it is true.

When I was growing up, we did not have a lot. The same is true for my wife. We remember what it was like. As parents with three kids, we had to wait to buy a second car—we simply didn't have the money at first. But that was okay. If I had to, I could go back and be poor again. My wife and I have had to do without before, and we could again if we had to. But for my kids, they have no memory of going without the way we had to. When young people have money troubles these days, their parents or grandparents can help them out if they choose to.

We recognize that money does not provide happiness, but it can make life easier when you have enough to pay your bills and buy food. The world is full of wealthy people who are miserable, however, and even wealthy people take their own lives tragically. I wish I could teach my children that money is important, but it is not the only source of happiness.

A Simple Budget Puts You in a Position of Strength

My whole philosophy in life and investment is *keep it simple, Stupid*—stupid being me. We need to keep things as simple as possible. I recognize what I recommend may seem so simple it cannot possibly work. But I want to return to the idea of spending less than you bring in. Budgeting is a great tool for keeping track.

At one point in my life, I was obese and then I lost one hundred pounds—this is how I did it. I said to myself: *Spencer, you can eat anything you want, but you have to write it down.*

I didn't want to write down the dozen doughnuts I ate, so I would not eat them. It is the same way with budgeting money. If you have to write down what you spend, you'll be less likely to spend it. If budgeting scares you, then do not budget. All you do is use your phone or a three-by-five card and write down every penny you spend. *Every penny you spend.*

How much are you spending at Starbucks?

Track it.

One man I worked with—he was twenty-seven years old—was spending an average of $220 per month at Starbucks. If he made his own coffee instead and put his coffee money into a basic mutual fund for the next thirty years, it would be worth over a million dollars. That's how getting control of wants versus needs and controlling ego will help us persistently and consistently spend less than we earn.

Implement a smart plan to invest and retire, so you never have to worry about outliving your money or running out. Or—heaven forbid—find yourself eighty years old and needing to rely on your children, or the government, or some other outside entity to provide for you. That is everything we are trying to avoid.

I recognize what I am suggesting sounds so simple; therefore, some people will not catch the vision of it. For those who are willing to learn—those who are willing to open their eyes and unplug their ears—this message can and will change their lives.

So my question for you, dear reader, is this: are you willing to change?

About the Author

Spencer Childs is an experienced retirement specialist and founder of Granite Financial, a Las-Vegas-based financial services firm. After his education at Brigham Young University, he enthusiastically began work as a financial professional. Throughout his thirty-year career, Spencer has been employed by three major firms and is the successful owner of a twenty-year-old private practice.

Spencer specializes in strategies designed to help prevent retirees from outliving their money. He has served hundreds of clients and handled millions of dollars' worth of financial assets. He applies his vast experience and knowledge to help individuals and families with their wealth preservation, retirement, insurance, and financial strategies with an emphasis on principal protection and tax-advantaged income solutions.

Retirement Planning Made Easy

by Frank C. Filisky

Prologue: Retirement is not a singular event; it's a journey. On average, it lasts twenty-one years, but to be safe, you need to plan for thirty, in case you're in the group that brings the average up. A comfortable retirement doesn't happen automatically because you simply want it to. There are too many challenges to overcome, any one of which can jeopardize the outcome desired. The key is to have a game plan in place before the journey starts.

An analogy I like to use is a sporting event. Several years ago, my daughter Stephanie announced that she was going to participate in triathlon events. To look at her, all five foot two inches, one hundred and twelve pounds, mother of three, in her mid-thirties, the obvious question was whether she'd be able to endure the mental and physical strain on her mind and body triathletes are put through.

After all, swimming two and a half miles, followed by a one-hundred-eighteen-mile bike ride, ending in a twenty-seven-mile run, all within the seventeen hours allotted, wouldn't be for the faint of heart.

She knew participating wasn't going to be a matter of just showing up. She had to train. She had to put together a game plan that prepared her for each event. She did her research and mapped out a training routine.

She began by taking a swimming lesson, followed by a schedule of swimming days. She bought a racing bike and went on all-day bike rides. Then she registered for and completed several marathons in the months leading up to the first triathlon. The only thing she couldn't plan for or control was the weather. It turned out weather did become an issue. In the first triathlon, it was bitterly cold. In the second triathlon, temperatures climbed to 115°F. Nine hundred of the thirty-one hundred participants representing fifty-two countries were forced to drop out due to heat exhaustion.

My daughter, to her credit, despite these adverse conditions, successfully completed both triathlons. No doubt, the key to her accomplishment was the planning and preparation she went through prior to the competition.

The planning that goes into a triathlon is parallel to planning for retirement. Each has their unique challenges and hurdles to overcome. In the case of retirement, several issues need to be confronted. There is ongoing inflation to contend with. A strategy must be in place to provide the extra income needed to be able to deal with the costs of goods and services that will likely double, and triple, over the course of time. The likelihood of stock market collapses will be unavoidable based upon history.

How will you be able to protect your retirement nest egg from being devastated?

Potential health issues could create additional expenses, possibly major additional expenses. Multiple senior research studies have shown that after age sixty-five, the probability that some form of health issue will appear is 70 percent.

The biggest challenge will be how to deal with the risk of longevity—living longer than initially planned for or expected. When polled, retirees state their number one fear is running out of money before they run out of retirement. Ironically, living too long could become a detriment rather than a blessing.

Retirement could still be everything you want it to be, if you are willing to take the time to develop a blueprint for taking action.

Accordingly, these next five steps will help you put everything into place.

Step One: Retirement Basics

Identify the three essential elements of a successful retirement:

1. Who are you planning for, and what do you have to work with in guaranteed income, savings, and investments?

2. What do you want, or perceive you need, in your retirement years?

3. What's your time frame to provide for these needs and wants?

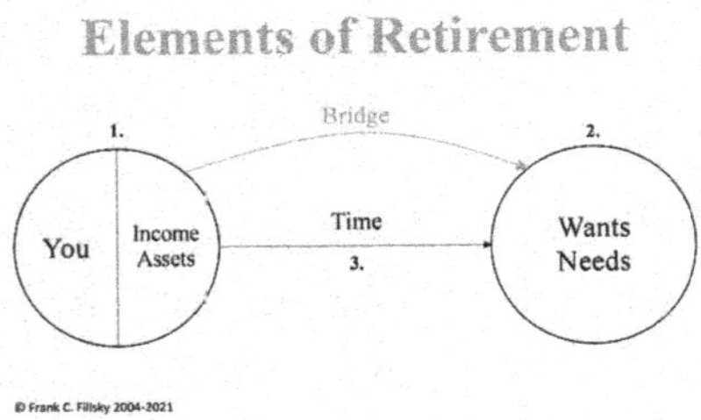

Once this information is in place, together we can build a bridge from where you are to where you want to be.

Step Two: Classifying Savings and Investments

Begin by pinpointing where savings and investments reside. The Menu of Investment Choices chart is excellent for this. The chart has two main categories, **Risky** and **Safe**. Each category is subdivided by its respective degree of risk and safety.

Once all savings and investments are listed by their classifications, each side of the equation is then totaled and converted into a percentage based against all assets. This gives an immediate picture of how much of all savings and investments, percentage-wise, are at risk and how much are not at risk and considered safe.

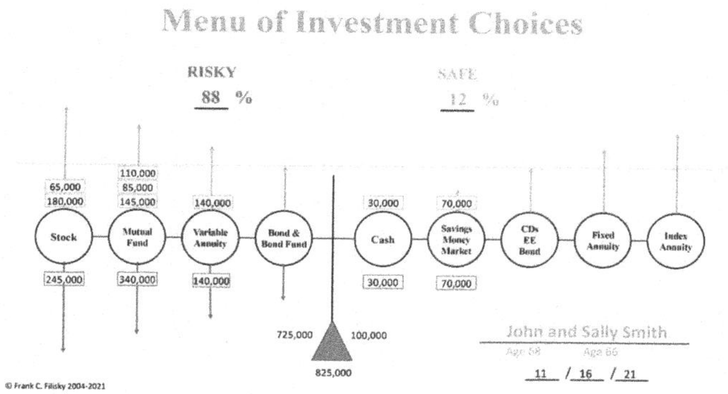

Are the current positions of savings and investment suitable for addressing overall needs for the years to come? That's the question to be answered.

Step Three: Suitability Tests

There are two fundamental money management rules to determine suitability and positioning of assets. They are *The Rule of 100* and *The Rule of 50 Percent*. These tests are conducted to see if assets are where they're supposed to be, according to levels of personal comfort and desired financial effectiveness.

The Rule of 100 determines how much of existing assets should be positioned on the Safe side of the equation and how much may be positioned on the Risky side of the equation.

Applying this rule, current age represents the percentage of how much existing assets should be in Safe categories. The difference between current age and 100 represents how much can then default to the Risky side of the equation. For example, a sixty-five-year-old should have 65 percent in categories on the Safe side and no more than 35 percent in categories on the Risky side.

The premise is that assets in Safe categories are shielded from loss and can therefore be counted on and their effectiveness controlled, whereas assets in Risky categories cannot be counted on, since they're vulnerable to loss. This distinction is important.

Billionaire Mark Cuban, when allowing his fortune to be managed by stockbrokers with their innate belief that they can always out-perform the market, came away with a telling quote I paraphrase here: "The market is a good place to make money; it is an even better place to lose it!" So much for the supreme confidence growth advisors have in their strategies.

If the percentages of asset placement do not match up according to The Rule of 100, then assets should be repositioned until they do.

When evaluating the assets on the Risky side, the second suitability test comes into play. The Rule of 50 Percent is an overlay to The Rule of 100 and only applies to the Risk categories. The assets in these categories should not be counted on over the long term if guarantees are needed or required. This is true because their performance will either produce substantially positive or negative results over the long haul, and their timing undo critical planning.

The 50 Percent Test consists of two questions whose answers illuminate the true levels of financial practicality and personal comfort suitability:

The first: *Can I afford to lose one half of what's here?*

If not, it's recommended that assets be moved to the Safe side until the answer becomes yes.

The second question: *Even if I can afford to lose one half of these assets, am I comfortable being left in that position?*

Again, if the answer is no, it's a sign that assets should be repositioned to the Safe side until the answer becomes yes.

A few years back, a new client, who had millions in pension money in the various Risky categories, a $250,000 salary, and a modest living standard of only $60,000 a year, was asked for her response to both questions. Yes was the answer to the first question. Since she was capable of adding another million dollars to her investments over the next five years, and she wouldn't be changing her modest lifestyle, she could afford to lose half her portfolio in the Risk categories. However, her answer was an emphatic no when it came to the second question. She had never paid attention to how much risk she was actually taking and what could happen based upon past market history.

Her feeling was that she worked hard to put the money aside, intending to pass it on to her family. She felt that before she allowed any external event to take that much value off her balance sheet, she would take everything out, pay the taxes, and give it to her two daughters and four granddaughters. The significance of that second test question completely turned around her resistance to change.

Applying these rules often contradicts the growth advisor's recommendations. Most advisors, if not all, are convinced that taking market risks will win out over time. It's been my experience that, regardless of age and circumstances, most growth advisors will put more than 90 percent of investments into Risky categories.

Their sense of diversification is to minimize the amount of risk by blending the options of low risk, medium risk, and high risk. Unfortunately, this keeps assets at risk and subject to loss.

For the investor, a better way to interpret their blending strategies is to understand what they truly mean.

The question one should ask is: *Do I want to lose a little bit of money (low risk), a lot of money (medium risk), or too much money (high risk)?*

Unfortunately, growth advisors don't offer a fourth option of: *I don't want to lose any money.*

Their option would refer to categories on the Safe side, which they rarely use or advocate.

It's important to understand and not lose sight of the fact that a successful retirement is built on income—income that is reliable, dependable, and, most importantly, sustainable.

Income is the outcome that matters most. Assets can be lost, stolen, mismanaged, divided in divorce, or devastated in the market. And the ongoing premise of the stock market is to grow assets through a gauntlet of risk. It was never conceived nor meant to provide the stable, consistent, guaranteed income that's required in retirement.

Only Safe categories are created and structured to provide the type of income that is needed at a time it is needed.

Step Four: Aligning Assets to Goals

What are the three stages of retirement that retirees will experience?

There's the *Now* . . . covering an investor's ages from their mid-sixties through their early seventies. This is when they are checking off what is in their Bucket List. It usually runs between twelve and fourteen years once retirement begins. It is also often referred to as the *GO-GO years.*

Next comes *Later* . . . mid-seventies to mid-eighties, when the Bucket List is about finished. Frequently referred to as the *SLOW-GO years.*

The third stage is *Much Later* . . . extending from the mid-eighties. This period is characterized by an attitude of, *I've been there, done that; not up to it* and tagged the *NO-GO years.*

An Emergency/Opportunity (E/O) fund is established above and beyond the standard income sources carrying the retiree through retirement. This fund has a dual purpose: First, to cover any unexpected expenses that may come up. And second, to provide a source of funds to cover the costs associated with opportunities the retirees should take advantage of when they occur. The size of the fund should be equivalent to one year of net income. For example, if a standard monthly overhead is net $4,000, then the fund should be at least $48,000 in size or more if desired.

The combination of locked-in income sources and an Emergency/Opportunity fund is designed to carry the retirees through the first stage of retirement, the GO-GO years.

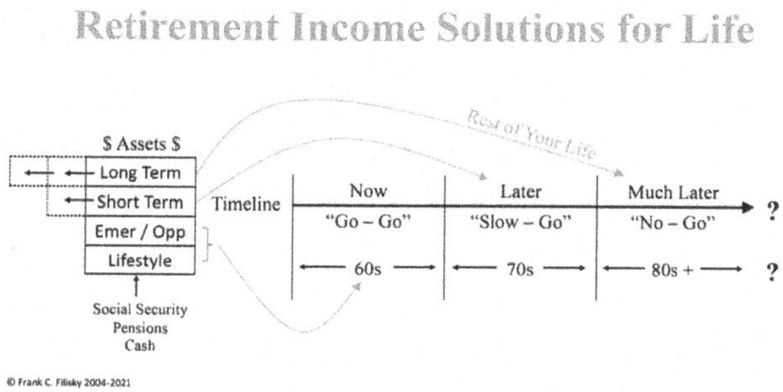

The balance of the remaining assets will be subdivided between the projected needs of the *later* stage and the *much later*, referred to as the *rest of their life period.*

Step Five: A Blueprint for Life

Goals have been confirmed. Available income and assets have been identified. Suitability tests have been run. And retirement time frames have been established. The final step is to tie everything together mathematically.

This is where computer software is used to create a composite lifetime blueprint of action to follow that takes retirees from their current ages up through age one hundred. Each year, the blueprint illustrates how income, assets, cash flow, taxes, inflation, market volatility, longevity, and legacy values are interfaced.

Frank C. Filisky, LLC

Retirement Income Solutions for Life

Planning Horizon: 36 yrs
Hypothetical Returns

			1 Private Pension - 401(k)		2 Honeywell Stock		3 Health Account Services		4 MM Checking		5 State Farm Annuity		6 LTC - 401(k)	
Year	Connie	Client2	Account	Income	Account	Income	Account	Income	Account	Income	Account	Income	Account	Income
net return	63	0	4.00 %	Connie IRA	0.00 %		0.00 %		1.00 %		1.00 %	Connie IRA	0.00 %	
init amount			150,000		8,618		45,379		12,475		51,279		153,702	
bonus %			0.00 %		0.00 %		0.00 %		0.00 %		0.00 %		20.00 %	
w/bonus			150,000		8,618		45,379		12,475		51,279		184,442	
end of 1	64	0	156,000	0	8,618	0	45,379	0	54,247	(41,648)	51,792	0	184,442	0
end of 2	65	0	162,240	0	8,618	0	45,379	0	95,483	(40,694)	52,310	0	184,442	0
end of 3	66	0	168,730	0	8,618	0	45,379	0	136,152	(39,714)	52,833	0	184,442	0
end of 4	67	0	175,479	0	8,618	0	45,379	0	176,220	(38,707)	53,361	0	184,442	0
end of 5	68	0	182,498	0	8,618	0	45,379	0	215,856	(37,673)	53,895	0	184,442	0
end of 6	69	0	189,798	0	8,618	0	45,379	0	246,656	(28,845)	54,434	0	184,442	0
end of 7	70	0	197,390	0	8,618	0	45,379	0	276,877	(27,754)	54,978	0	184,442	0
end of 8	71	0	205,285	0	8,618	0	45,379	0	275,945	3,701	55,528	0	184,442	0
end of 9	72	0	213,497	0	8,618	0	45,379	0	273,844	4,860	56,083	0	184,442	0
end of 10	73	0	222,037	0	8,618	0	45,379	0	270,531	6,051	56,644	0	184,442	0
end of 11	74	0	230,918	0	8,618	0	45,379	0	264,302	8,934	57,210	0	184,442	0
end of 12	75	0	240,155	0	8,618	0	45,379	0	256,795	10,191	57,782	0	184,442	0
end of 13	76	0	249,761	0	8,618	0	45,379	0	247,841	11,481	58,360	0	184,442	0
end of 14	77	0	242,014	17,737	8,618	0	45,379	0	265,251	(4,931)	58,944	0	184,442	0
end of 15	78	0	233,958	17,737	8,618	0	45,379	0	261,374	(3,670)	59,533	0	184,442	0
end of 16	79	0	225,579	17,737	8,618	0	45,379	0	236,610	27,377	60,129	0	184,442	0
end of 17	80	0	216,865	17,737	8,618	0	45,379	0	210,164	28,812	60,730	0	184,442	0
end of 18	81	0	207,803	17,737	8,618	0	45,379	0	181,979	30,286	61,337	0	184,442	0
end of 19	82	0	198,378	17,737	8,618	0	45,379	0	151,999	31,800	61,951	0	184,442	0
end of 20	83	0	188,576	17,737	8,618	0	45,379	0	120,164	33,355	62,570	0	184,442	0
end of 21	84	0	178,382	17,737	8,618	0	45,379	0	86,415	34,951	63,196	0	184,442	0
end of 22	85	0	167,781	17,737	8,618	0	45,379	0	50,689	36,590	63,828	0	184,442	0
end of 23	86	0	156,755	17,737	8,618	0	45,379	0	12,923	38,273	64,466	0	184,442	0
end of 24	87	0	145,288	17,737	8,618	0	45,379	0	0	13,052	65,111	0	184,442	0
end of 25	88	0	133,362	17,737	8,618	0	45,379	0	0	0	65,762	0	184,442	0
end of 26	89	0	120,960	17,737	8,618	0	45,379	0	0	0	66,419	0	184,442	0
end of 27	90	0	108,061	17,737	8,618	0	45,379	0	0	0	67,084	0	184,442	0
end of 28	91	0	94,647	17,737	8,618	0	45,379	0	0	0	67,754	0	184,442	0
end of 29	92	0	80,696	17,737	8,618	0	45,379	0	0	0	68,432	0	184,442	0
end of 30	93	0	66,186	17,737	8,618	0	45,379	0	0	0	69,116	0	184,442	0
end of 31	94	0	51,097	17,737	8,618	0	45,379	0	0	0	69,807	0	184,442	0
end of 32	95	0	35,404	17,737	8,618	0	45,379	0	0	0	70,506	0	184,442	0
end of 33	96	0	19,083	17,737	8,618	0	45,379	0	0	0	71,211	0	184,442	0
end of 34	97	0	2,106	17,737	8,618	0	45,379	0	0	0	71,923	0	184,442	0
end of 35	98	0	0	17,737	8,618	0	45,379	0	0	0	72,642	0	184,442	0
end of 36	99	0	0	17,737	8,618	0	45,379	0	0	0	73,368	0	184,442	0
				407,991		0		0		56,180		0		0

	7 Account Balance	8 Structured Income	9	10	11	12	13	14	15	16	17	18	19 Targets	20
Year	Accounts Total	Planned Dist.	Connie SS (9)	Connie Pension (9)	Allianz (18)	Allianz (19)	Allianz (20)	Global Atlantic (6)	State Farm (6)	Church Bonds (6)	Fed + State	After Tax Income	After Tax Target	Income Gap
net return														
init amount	421,453	subtotal												from total
bonus %	30,740	of account	Infl Factor	Infl Factor	Infl Factor	Infl Factor	Infl Factor	Infl Factor	Infl Factor	Infl Factor	Tax Rate		Infl Factor	income to
w/bonus	452,193	incomes	2.00 %	0.00 %	0.00 %	0.00 %	0.00 %	0.00 %	0.00 %	0.00 %	13.00 %		2.50 %	target
end of 1	500,479	(41,648)	21,264	3,828	566	1,660	7,200	29,908	2,844	29,550	(7,172)	48,000	48,000	0
end of 2	548,470	(40,694)	21,689	3,828	566	1,660	7,200	29,908	2,844	29,550	(7,352)	49,200	49,200	0
end of 3	596,154	(39,714)	22,123	3,828	566	1,660	7,200	29,908	2,844	29,550	(7,536)	50,430	50,430	0
end of 4	643,499	(38,707)	22,566	3,828	566	1,660	7,200	29,908	2,844	29,550	(7,724)	51,691	51,691	0
end of 5	690,487	(37,673)	23,017	3,828	566	1,660	7,200	29,908	2,844	29,550	(7,917)	52,983	52,983	0
end of 6	729,327	(28,845)	23,477	3,828	0	1,660	0	29,908	2,844	29,550	(8,115)	54,308	54,308	0
end of 7	767,684	(27,754)	23,947	3,828	0	1,660	0	29,908	2,844	29,550	(8,318)	55,665	55,665	0
end of 8	775,197	3,701	24,000	3,828	0	1,660	0	0	2,844	29,550	(8,526)	57,057	57,057	0
end of 9	781,363	4,860	24,480	3,828	0	1,660	0	0	2,844	29,550	(8,739)	58,483	58,483	0
end of 10	787,651	6,051	24,970	3,828	0	1,660	0	0	2,844	29,550	(8,957)	59,945	59,945	0
end of 11	790,870	8,934	25,469	3,828	0	0	0	0	2,844	29,550	(9,181)	61,444	61,444	0
end of 12	793,121	10,191	25,978	3,828	0	0	0	0	2,844	29,550	(9,411)	62,980	62,980	0
end of 13	794,402	11,481	26,498	3,828	0	0	0	0	2,844	29,550	(9,646)	64,555	64,555	0
end of 14	794,648	12,806	27,028	3,828	0	0	0	0	2,844	29,550	(9,887)	66,169	66,169	0
end of 15	793,304	14,167	27,568	3,828	0	0	0	0	2,844	29,550	(10,134)	67,823	67,823	0
end of 16	760,757	45,114	28,120	3,828	0	0	0	0	2,844	0	(10,388)	69,518	69,518	0
end of 17	726,198	46,560	28,682	3,828	0	0	0	0	2,844	0	(10,647)	71,256	71,256	0
end of 18	689,550	48,023	29,256	3,828	0	0	0	0	2,844	0	(10,914)	73,038	73,038	0
end of 19	650,767	49,537	29,841	3,828	0	0	0	0	2,844	0	(11,187)	74,864	74,864	0
end of 20	609,750	51,092	30,438	3,828	0	0	0	0	2,844	0	(11,466)	76,735	76,735	0
end of 21	566,432	52,688	31,047	3,828	0	0	0	0	2,844	0	(11,753)	78,654	78,654	0
end of 22	520,737	54,327	31,667	3,828	0	0	0	0	2,844	0	(12,047)	80,620	80,620	0
end of 23	472,883	56,010	32,301	3,828	0	0	0	0	2,844	0	(12,348)	82,636	82,636	0
end of 24	448,838	30,789	32,947	3,828	0	0	0	0	2,844	0	(9,153)	61,255	84,701	(23,447)
end of 25	437,564	17,737	33,606	3,828	0	0	0	0	2,844	0	(7,542)	50,473	86,819	(36,346)
end of 26	425,819	17,737	34,278	3,828	0	0	0	0	2,844	0	(7,629)	51,058	88,989	(37,932)
end of 27	413,584	17,737	34,963	3,828	0	0	0	0	2,844	0	(7,716)	51,654	91,214	(39,560)
end of 28	400,841	17,737	35,663	3,828	0	0	0	0	2,844	0	(7,809)	52,262	93,494	(41,232)
end of 29	387,567	17,737	36,376	3,828	0	0	0	0	2,844	0	(7,902)	52,883	95,832	(42,949)
end of 30	373,742	17,737	37,104	3,828	0	0	0	0	2,844	0	(7,997)	53,516	98,227	(44,712)
end of 31	359,344	17,737	37,846	3,828	0	0	0	0	2,844	0	(8,093)	54,161	100,683	(46,522)
end of 32	344,349	17,737	38,602	3,828	0	0	0	0	2,844	0	(8,191)	54,820	103,200	(48,380)
end of 33	328,733	17,737	39,375	3,828	0	0	0	0	2,844	0	(8,292)	55,492	105,780	(50,288)
end of 34	312,471	17,737	40,162	3,828	0	0	0	0	2,844	0	(8,394)	56,177	108,425	(52,248)
end of 35	311,081	17,737	40,965	3,828	0	0	0	0	2,844	0	(8,499)	56,876	111,135	(54,260)
end of 36	311,806	17,737	41,785	3,828	0	0	0	0	2,844	0	(8,606)	57,588	113,914	(56,325)
		464,131	1,089,096	137,808	2,830	16,600	36,000	209,356	102,384	443,250	(325,189)	2,176,266	2,750,466	(574,200)

Important Note - the values shown on the Structured Income Plan in orange are hypothetical returns.

MARKET PROTECTION INCLUDED

LONG TERM CARE COVERAGE INCLUDED

Structured Lifetime Income Plan: Connie [redacted]

Prepared By: Frank C. Filisky, CFP

Summary: Whether you are about to take on the rigors of a triathlon or planning your retirement, success is guaranteed only if you plan ahead and follow your plan.

About the Author

Frank C. Filisky's company, Frank C. Filisky, LLC, provides comprehensive financial and tax planning advice to retirees. As the Safe Money Experts, they design and implement retirement income programs for their clients.

Academically, Frank earned the prestigious designations of Certified Financial Planner (CFP*), Certified Estate Planner (CEP*), Chartered Financial Consultant (ChFC*), and Chartered Life Underwriter (CLU*). He's a member of the Financial Planning Association, the Society of Financial Service Professionals, and the Society of Estate Planners. His undergraduate degrees are in Business and Psychology from Youngstown State University.

Frank has been interviewed regarding his expertise on ABC, NBC, CBS, and FOX as well as being featured in *Kiplinger's* magazine regarding retirement planning for Ohioans.

Community-wise, Frank served on the Board of Directors of Eastern Mental Health Center and Consumer Credit Counseling, a service he helped originate.

In his village of Lowellville, Frank served as Tax Commissioner, the high school's statistician for football and basketball, and as a sports columnist covering these same events for the local newspaper.

Develop a Retirement Plan for Owner Success

by Dave Loskill

People spend more time planning their vacation than they do planning their retirement. They have absolutely no road map of how to reach the retirement goals they set for themselves. Many people have no idea what income they'll require throughout their retirement years, nor do they understand how the assets they've accumulated through the Wall Street casino—Wall Street *is* a casino—will work together to help them accomplish their retirement goals. Wall Street has no real distribution plan for how your accumulation will last you for the rest of your lifetime.

When designing your Retirement Road Map, it is best to work with people who know and understand how to design and construct a road map for actual retirement plans that make retirement life better and more successful. People nearing retirement or in retirement should not be using the *wish in one hand and hope in the other* approach to planning. Neither one is going to work very well. So we ensure people understand, more than anything, that without a Road Map to Retirement Success, part of your retirement may end up with a *J-O-B*, which, we say in retirement, stands for *Just Over Broke*. Because the reason you would come out of retirement and go back to work is you had a hope and a prayer rather than a plan and a strategy. And we think it is vital for every person approaching or in retirement to develop a plan and a strategy.

A Road Map to Retirement Success

It is estimated that only 40 percent of Americans have an actual, drafted, written plan of how their assets will work together to ensure a successful retirement plan.

An optimal plan should include:

- Social security
- Pension
- 401(k)
- IRA
- 403(b)
- 457
- Manage money
- Rental properties
- Returns on these investments

The key is putting these elements together in a written format you can follow, one we can assess and adjust every year. With an actual, written, developed retirement plan, you can figure out how these assets can work in unison rather than randomly draw from one resource with no knowledge of how it may hurt you in another.

Of the 40 percent of people who have a written road map to financial success, half do not believe it will work. Those are staggering numbers. People are uncomfortable today in retirement because of circumstances within our government and in the world. Many retirees are reevaluating what they thought would last them the rest of their lifetime.

Your Road Map to Retirement Success should include contingencies for the unexpected—when you don't know what tomorrow brings, you should prepare for whatever you foresee. A good plan successfully plans for obstacles. If the obstacles we anticipate never come about, the plan provides a better retirement for the person, not a worse one.

You should be able to pull your road map out at a moment's notice, look at it, and say: *I am right on track*, or *I am not*. When you consult your road map, it should show you exactly where you thought you were going to be at any given point in your retirement.

Throw the Kitchen Sink at It!

We cannot accurately predict everything that will occur during your retirement. However, we know how to help you create the best plan possible. That involves drawing on all our knowledge, expertise, and resources.

When developing your retirement plan, use everything, *including* the kitchen sink, and consider the following factors:

1. **Worst-case scenarios**. Put your retirement plan through every possible scenario of what may go wrong in your retirement. If you say: *I need five thousand dollars a month in net income*, and net income is what you can spend each month, that is always the number that we start the plan with. Remember, you need that for the rest of your life.

2. **Inflation**. Factor in 3 percent for inflation every year for the rest of your lifetime. If you do not, twenty years from now, that $5,000 per month must increase by 60 percent just for you to continue to live the same lifestyle you are living right now.

3. **Social security**. Social security is a huge building block in your retirement plan. Always work with someone who is considered an expert on the subject. There are 567 ways to claim social security. There are over 2,000 rules that govern it and over 100,000 program operating manual systems. The way you draw on your social security can cost you hundreds of thousands of dollars if not done correctly.

   Have you looked at the possibility of using a *start, stop, start* strategy with your social security, in which you start the benefit, collect it for a few years, and then turn it off?

Your social security grows by 6.7 percent each year that you are not taking it from age sixty-two to sixty-six. And from sixty-six to seventy, it grows at 8 percent. We may decide to turn it on early, when your other assets are growing at a greater accumulation than what social security is. Then, when your assets are not accumulating gains as much as social security is, you suspend your benefit, let it accumulate at the 8 percent rate, and reactivate it at 70 years of age and benefit from the increased income for the rest of your lifetime.

For the last ten years, social security has been telling the American public that, in 2035, every single American social security benefit is going to be reduced by 21 percent.

What are you going to do when your social security is reduced by 21 percent? Have you prepared for this? It should be in every retirement plan, assuming you have one. Not to anticipate this obstacle in your plan is committing fiduciary financial malpractice.

4. **Death.** Are you incorporating death in your long-term plan? It is an essential factor.

   What income stream will replace the lost income that occurs when one of your loved ones passes away?

And do not say *life insurance*, because the majority of all life insurance policies never pay a benefit. The average man lives to eighty-six, and the average woman lives until eighty-eight. We plan for death so when someone dies, the surviving loved ones have sufficient funds to live on.

Have you taken into consideration what is going to happen to your tax bracket when your spouse passes away? Because it is going to double; you will no longer be able to file as "married filing jointly." You will be single. Will you lose a pension income? You're going to lose at least one social security income. Does it affect any payouts from your IRA or managed assets portfolios? These are all very important items that must be addressed in the Road Map to Retirement Success.

5. **Market changes.** All retirement plans should include at least two major downturns in the stock market to show how the plan will weather market losses and show the effects they will have on your retirement plans. Planning for at least two 50 percent drops in the market over a twenty-five-year retirement truly stress-tests any retirement plan.

Throwing the kitchen sink at your retirement plan allows you to know whether it will allow you to live the life you want to live in retirement.

Build a Strong Foundation

We start our lives in an *accumulation phase*. The investment expert you work with during that phase is much different from the person you should be working with as you approach and are in the retirement phase. In the accumulation phase, the goal is growth. A distribution or retirement planning expert's goal is making sure your money lasts the rest of your life.

AARP states in their magazine that every year for the last ten years, the number one fear shared by people approaching retirement or in retirement is that they are going to run out of money before they run out of life.

A good Road Map to Retirement Success also considers:

- Which asset will grow better?
- If you own a rental property, what condition is it in? How long do you want to keep fixing pipes and cleaning toilets and replacing broken windows?
- How will taxes affect your plan?
- Are you working until sixty-five only because you need medical care?

Having an advisor who is an expert in retirement planning means knowing and understanding how programs like this can be used. Are you aware that we can work into the plan the Affordable Care Act (ACA), by structuring your income so that you can qualify for free and good healthcare until you reach Medicare age? That's because nowhere in the ACA does it ask how much money you *have*. It asks you how much money you *make*. Knowing this difference allows a retirement planning professional to structure an income plan to keep your reportable income at a level that allows you to qualify for free health care and live the life you want to live in retirement without having to work until Medicare age.

By structuring your assets together, using Roth or Nonqualified Assets or Non Reportable Assets, we can structure a plan in which you retire early, have medical insurance paid for by the government, and achieve the financial goals you want to achieve.

For your other assets, we examine their historical rates of return and the level of safety you are comfortable with now versus the levels when you were twenty, thirty, or forty. I think everybody would have to agree we tend to have a different outlook on this stuff as we get older. I am sure there are people who are still happy getting 30 or 40 percent. But as we approach retirement, the goal is to not lose what we already have, so we don't have to go and get that J-O-B.

But remember: the greater the return, the greater the risk.

If you are drawing on your market-based assets to fund your retirement, the market has a major correction, and you have to keep drawing on that asset, and you will never, ever, recuperate. It is called the *Sequence of Returns*. There have been hundreds of papers written about it, but they all say the same thing. You cannot continue to draw on an asset and expect it to last your entire lifetime if the asset is experiencing losses due to market corrections. Also, if the correction happens early in your retirement, it is worse than if a crash happens later in your retirement.

All Road Maps to Retirement Success should plan for long-term care needs. One excellent way to do this is to set up a self-funding pension, in which the income stream can double if you meet two of six activities of daily life. There is no medical physical involved in obtaining these types of policies, and medical history plays no role. If you have not considered these types, it may be time for you to sit down with a professional retirement distribution expert. They can show you how putting all your assets together can accomplish your retirement goals.

Monte Carlo **Your Options**

Monte Carlo is probably one the greatest gambling areas in the world. Most of us cannot afford simply walking into a place like that because of the costs for the tables and everything else. But when we say *Monte Carlo* your options, we mean to run multiple scenarios for your retirement plan to see what combination of using your assts works the best for your Road Map to Retirement Success.

For example, what if:

- You begin collecting social security at sixty-two and your spouse collects at sixty-seven?
- You use the start-stop-start strategy and put a stop to collecting at age sixty-seven, and do not restart your benefit until you are seventy?
- You draw down on one asset, then shut off that asset, and draw down another?
- You pledge a certain amount of money to a long-term income plan, which you know will grow 8 percent every year with compounded interest, and then activate it for income?

Every financial vehicle, my friends, has a flaw in it. You can work with your financial planner to plot and graph how multiple plans compare to one another. It is an incredible way to see how making one slight change can totally change the course of your retirement.

You may wish to develop the various scenarios, including what happens if:

- You are obliged to take the money as income, such as RMDs.
- Spouses collect social security at different times.

- The market corrects at various times during your retirement years.
- You or your spouse require long-term care.
- Five years into the plan, you need a new car.
- You want to downsize and move into a smaller home.
- You want to leave a legacy for children or inheritors.

Everybody is different, and circumstances are likely to change over time. So, work with your advisor to explore different scenarios. Without doing this, you are shooting in the dark or driving without a map. Nobody goes on vacation without GPS or a map. You need to be shown multiple retirement plans to learn the best way to accomplish your goals.

Constantly Update Your Road Map

Every advisor should sit down with their client at least once a year—maybe over a piece of pie and a cup of coffee—and update their road map for financial retirement success. During the course of that year, much as you may like your investment advisor, you probably have not seen or talked with them about your accounts.

Their responsibility as a fiduciary is to look out for you.

What have you done that you haven't told your investment advisor about or is not on the plan?

You are not a little kid. You do not have to ask your investment advisor *permission* to do anything. They may not give you any pie because you did it, but they can update the plan to adjust for the changes you have made. What happens if clients come in saying they've sold their home and are going to buy a $300,000 Winnebago, and for the next three years they're going to drive around the United States? That was not in the original plan.

Does it mean they cannot do it?

No, it means we must update their plan, considering questions, such as:

- How does making a major change to the plan like that effect the overall appearance and the future of the plan?
- What has happened in the last year in the market to the assets that were exposed?
- Is social security really going to reduce benefits by 21 percent? As we get closer, we will know.

If your investment advisor is not updating your plan, they are committing fiduciary malpractice. They have an obligation to look out for you and update those plans every year. They may call you to come in and sit down. And you may say, "No, thanks; everything is going great." Well, they cannot force you. But it is a mistake not to review your plans annually.

I hope you realize it is worth a couple of hours once a year over a piece of pie and a cup of coffee to make sure that the road map that has been created for your retirement financial success gets you to the pot of gold you dream of.

About the Author

The Loskill Financial Group represents a major part of the life work of Dave and GayLynn Loskill. Dave and GayLynn have been together in business and in life for over three decades, and they have always worked toward the central goal of assisting others and transforming the dreams of their customers into reality. Dave and GayLynn have been extremely successful in helping others achieve what they most want out of their lives—their practice is now ranked in the top five nationally at Tucker Advisors. They both sit on the Tucker Advisory Board, assisting other advisors around the country with their practices. They possess the relevant, one-stop-shop licensing to handle all the financial needs of their clients, including Series 65, Medicare, Long-Term Care, and multiple insurance licenses. They are experts in the field of retirement income planning.

They are able to produce complete retirement income plans for their clients that include all aspects of their financial future for them: complete legacy planning, trusts, social security, and so on. They are licensed in managed money, Long-Term Care, and life insurance. Everything is under one roof.

With their home and hearts deeply rooted in the state of Arizona for over fifty years, they are dedicated to the community they work in and serve. They love spending time outdoors in the beautiful Arizona climate. Dave is also recognized as one of Arizona's top wrestling officials, having officiated across the state for more than thirty-five years, as well as officiating for the state championships for the last ten years. GayLynn graduated from Arizona State University with a bachelor's degree in Accounting. She went on to obtain her CPA license and worked in public accounting for ten years, specializing in audit and financial accounting. Together, GayLynn and Dave have given away the Loskill Financial Academic Scholarship to a deserving student athlete in Arizona for more than a decade.

Dave and GayLynn have two sons, Carl and Christopher, and two daughters, Nichole and Morganne, and are expecting their first grandchild.

Family, good values, and assisting others have always been and will continue to be the driving forces that motivate Dave and GayLynn in their business and personal lives. As Christians, they are very involved in their church and in their community. They also believe in dedicating their time to volunteering at their local church, spending time weekly in Bible study, and striving always to follow the Lord. They work with the homeless through the Agape House and work with the Salvation Army.

Dave and Gaylnn welcome the opportunity to get to know you—and to show you how they can assist you and your family achieve your financial dreams.

Healthcare Through Retirement

by Michael Riley

I have been a financial planner for over thirty years, and it still amazes me how one critical aspect of an individual's retirement plan continues to be overlooked. Many planners will discuss investment, taxes, and estate planning, but few address healthcare through retirement. There is a misconception that sources such as Medicare or Medicaid will cover all medical expenses at the age of sixty-five. Yet, there are many expenses that require additional resources or private insurance.

During our initial interview with new clients, we discover that they already have different investment strategies in place, such as life insurance, 401(k)s, IRAs, Roth IRAs, and maybe some miscellaneous legal documentation. Many people focus on the financial aspects of their plan and how their investments will sustain their lifestyle through retirement without considering that this will include their need for healthcare.

As individuals age, they should have a deeper understanding of their future healthcare needs and include these in a comprehensive retirement plan.

One can easily set aside funds for their monthly income and expenses, but what happens when something unexpected arises with their ability to perform daily activities?

Many assume that a chronic illness will incur greater expenses than a longer life expectancy. In the short term, this might be the case, but total healthcare costs will be more likely to increase as individuals grow into their nineties.

Some things to take into consideration today are:

- Your current health
- Your previous medical history
- Your biological parents' health

A most desirable situation would be to maintain healthcare while still living at home. However, this is not always the ideal situation. The cost of coordinating and receiving care at home could be overwhelming and expensive. Therefore, a transition would have to be considered if an individual's health is compromised.

We understand that along with this difficult transition will come an emotional one. Imagine, for a moment, being surrounded by all the comforts of home, with treasured items in every room. Then, think about having to move into a much smaller environment in an unfamiliar community.

What if you could make this transition easier on yourself, your family, and your loved ones?

Replacing this burden with proper planning will eliminate much of the anxiety that comes with making this transition. Along with allocating the funds to make this move possible, one may want to consider taking care of their personal possessions. Throughout life, we accumulate a lot of things, many of them with sentimental value: our wedding gifts, old china, possibly even some of our children's belongings. We can't possibly take all of that with us!

Building Financial Security Around Healthcare

It is essential to make sure there is access to reliable funds that will pay for healthcare as you age. Let me tell you a story about one of our clients. Several years ago, we worked with a husband and wife who had accumulated a sum of $5 million. The husband was a doctor, while the wife took care of the house and children. During his working years, the majority of their assets was in three different properties: his office, their home, and an additional investment property they owned.

Upon his retirement in 2008, there was only enough income for this couple to cover their monthly expenses.

Do you remember the great recession during this time?

His property value depreciated and there was a lack in buyers. This is when the real estate market plummeted and the lack of liquidity from their property made it very difficult for them to pay for his healthcare expenses as his health began to decline. Eventually, my clients didn't have a choice other than to liquidate their investment property at less than 50 percent of its value.

Had this couple come to visit with us earlier, we could have helped avoid such an unfortunate situation. By exploring different options to provide a plan with a written strategy, an individual can feel confident knowing that they will be able to overcome the unexpected.

Creating a Legal Plan

A good friend of mine works in the emergency room in the retirement community of Sun City Center. Over dinner one night, he shared a story about a patient who was hospitalized for a stroke. Sadly, her spouse had passed away a year earlier and her next of kin was a daughter who lived in Maine. Because of the stroke, the patient was unable to communicate, and the doctor could not talk with her.

When he was finally able to contact her daughter, he said, "I want to let you know your mom had a stroke and I need to talk to you as her healthcare surrogate. We need to discuss options to treat her, but before I do that, I need a copy of your healthcare surrogate document."

The daughter responded, "Mom has one of those at her home in Sun City Center. I can't access it right now, and I am not sure how quickly I can get down there."

Unfortunately, the doctor was unable to discuss his patient's healthcare needs without proof of legal documentation.

So many times, we meet with new clients who don't have their legal documents in order. The documents are either outdated or have been drafted in a different state and are invalid.

The three important documents to have readily available are:

- Durable power of attorney
- Health care surrogate
- Living will

It is critical to have these documents current and in proper order as part of a well-devised estate plan. Someone must be appointed to direct your healthcare and financial decisions in the event you are unable to. We feel strongly about clients creating a legal plan that ultimately helps make decisions easier in a time of need.

Preparing for Transition

It is usually the children who first notice their parent is beginning to slow down. They notice that their parent is no longer able to do everything they were once very capable of doing. These things may include general housekeeping, cooking, lawn care, driving, or keeping up with their finances.

While parents are more than likely aware of their shortcomings, they may find it difficult to admit them in fear of losing their independence and putting a burden on their children. At the same time, the children are concerned with the changes that are happening and want to protect their parents. However, many children are living in a different state or are unable be present every day because they may have the responsibility of their own family or a demanding job.

At times, children of our clients will come in and ask us to help them and their parents understand the transition into an independent or assisted living facility. These options can contribute to the family's well-being because they may lessen the responsibility on the parents, as well as ease the pressure off the children. These facilities provide the necessary interaction and activities, fresh and well-balanced meals, cleaning services, and healthcare services. Once in facilities such as these, the parents are no longer isolated. They are safe and become part of a community.

Many clients are enjoying their retirement in places such as these because they are able to dedicate their time participating in the activities they enjoy rather than dealing with the stress of maintaining a home.

This transition is one of the most difficult to make, for both the retirees entering a new home and their loved ones who assist them. However, after the three to six months we label as *a period of adjustment*, many families are dealing with it well and wonder why they didn't do it sooner. Our commitment to our clients is not only to see them to retirement, but to walk alongside them as they enter the different phases of their journey.

Understanding Levels of Care

Most people are familiar with the government's health insurance program, Medicare. Once an individual reaches the age of sixty-five, they become eligible for this program. In addition, a supplemental program may be purchased to cover the 20 percent that Medicare Part A and Part B do not cover. Medical Advantage programs are also available to replace Medicare Part A, Part B, and the supplement and involve some type of copay. All these programs are limited in coverage of long-term care expenses.

Depending on the facility and state, the average cost of living in an independent facility can range from $2,000 to $5,000 per month.

Independent living facilities typically offer:

- Meals
- Utilities
- Housekeeping
- Scheduled transportation

They may have staff on site to monitor the facility, but they do not provide medication management or personal assistance.

Assisted living care facilities, on the other hand, offer:

- Meals
- Utilities
- Housekeeping
- Scheduled transportation
- Personal assistance with self-care
- Medication management
- Health monitoring
- Trained care associates

Depending on the level of assistance needed, the average cost can range between $4,500 to $8,000 per month. The twenty-four-hour care offered at these facilities can provide security and peace of mind for clients and their families. Although many children have the desire to care for their parents as they age, they may not fully understand the amount of commitment and responsibility it may take until the time comes. In many cases, they just won't have access to the resources necessary to care for their parents in a respectful and dignified manner. If a retirement plan includes these potential types of expenses, this stage of life could be more appropriately managed.

One afternoon, I received a phone call from a client's daughter who asked for my advice on having her widowed mother move in with her. She had a young family with three school-aged children and assisted her husband with running his small business. Her mother was only seventy-one years old, but had a few health concerns such as arthritis, asthma, digestive issues, and difficulty walking without assistance. The mother used a walker most of the time, but needed to use her scooter when she wasn't well.

The daughter in this case was more than willing to do all she could for her mother and felt like she was perfectly capable. As her mother was living on her own, among other tasks, she would do some light cleaning around the house, assist her in shopping, take her to medical appointments and provide companionship when time allowed her to get away.

The more she spoke to me, the more I could sense resentment in her voice. It sounded like this mother-daughter relationship was being strained because of what they both were going through. Her mother wanted her independence even though her abilities were declining, and the daughter wanted to care for her mother, but was feeling the resistance along with the stress due to all the time and energy her mother required. She already had her home and family responsibilities, not to mention her individual needs.

Upon listening to her concerns, I offered some feedback. She began to consider the benefits of moving her mother into an independent living facility. Although her mother was resistant in the beginning, the transition was a positive one, and the two began to enjoy their time together.

The daughter can rest at ease, knowing that her mother is surrounded by other like-minded people and is part of a community that provides activities and recreation to keep her active. The apartment in the facility was much easier to move in with the walker, and the meals provided were healthy and sustainable. She had never imagined herself enjoying her time like that. Without the help of her daughter and the proper planning, financially and emotionally, this may not have gone so smoothly.

How to Pay for It All

Ideally, individuals should meet with a financial planner before their retirement years. A comprehensive evaluation of your health concerns should be prepared. Taking longevity into account, we will identify assets that may be set aside for potential healthcare expenses. These assets can be invested in a variety of ways and should have the ability to be liquidated in case the need arises.

This is considered an individual being self-insured. The individual maintains control of the assets and chooses where they will receive care, paying out of pocket for medical costs. Paying out of retirement dollars might not be the best choice as the consequences could include unfavorable taxes. There is also the potential to run out of money if you incur greater than expected costs.

Traditional long-term care insurance is another option one may consider. This type of insurance may cover your core costs, but it can be expensive, and the premium is not guaranteed. The potential increase in premium also creates uncertainty with your finances. It is also important to consider the possibility of paying into a program like this and not being able to reap the benefits, whether due to a sudden accident or unforeseen health reasons.

New hybrid plans are replacing long-term care policies. These hybrid plans include long-term care riders that are attached to the life insurance policy. Individuals would invest a sum of money, and if this funding is not needed for healthcare costs, a death benefit is paid out to the beneficiary. However, if this funding proves necessary, the amount paid out will be reduced.

In many instances, these hybrid plans are more beneficial than some of the traditional long-term care policies that individuals continue to pay into for years. The premiums paid toward long-term care policies are lost in the event of a sudden death. One must also take into account that the traditional healthcare policies may increase over time.

The long-term hybrid approach is one way for an individual to gain peace of mind. They know their estate will not be eroded. They know they will not be robbed of all they worked hard for. It will transfer to their beneficiaries, leaving a legacy.

About the Author

Michael Riley is the CEO of Estate and Retirement Resources, Inc. He founded Estate and Retirement Resources, Inc. in 1998 with the intent of creating an unrivaled experience for his clients. Since that time, Michael has strived to become a highly distinguished Financial Planner. His impressive list of accreditations includes CFP®, CLU®, and ChFC®. In addition to Estate and Retirement Planning, he specializes in creating Wealth Management Strategies customized for each individual.

Michael's success is due to his superior attentiveness to each client's individual needs. His remarkable reputation has granted him the honor of being entrusted with the transition of his clients' accounts from one generation to another.

Michael lives in Florida with his wife and four children where, as a tight-knit family, they care for his mother and mother-in-law. He enjoys spending time watching the sunsets along the beautiful Gulf Coast beaches with his family, sports, reading, and serving his community. He serves on multiple boards, including the Salvation Army.

Keep More of Your Money With Smart Tax Planning

by Kenneth Tumolo

If you retire at sixty-five, do you have enough to live on through your eighties?

Tax planning can help both those who have saved enough and those who haven't. A good plan includes considerations for when to draw Social Security, how to draw on different accounts, estate planning, and how to reduce taxes so you can keep more money in your pocket. No one wants to pay the IRS or their state extra money—we make sure it stays with you so you can use it to live your fullest life in retirement, pass it along to your family, or donate it to a charity.

People consult me because they have been retired five years or so, and they've discovered a problem in their current plan. I can see the core of their problem is they did not adequately plan. They are missing the tax strategies that give them an advantage. For these people, I wish I had met them five or six years ago, when they first went into retirement. I could have done so much more for them, guiding them, especially regarding taxation. In past years, they may have paid more than they should have on taxes, and the IRS isn't going to call them to give their money back. They made the choice to draw the way they did; it is on them. The other pieces usually fall into place.

Often when I review their plans, I see they could have saved thousands of dollars if they had structured their plan just a little differently right from the beginning of their retirement. This is why it's vital to start your planning early. Most people really dig in only six months or a year before retirement. Some people start planning five years early. You should start as early as possible, which gives you more options for planning. Your plan becomes more and more important the closer you get. The longer we have to implement a plan and follow through with it, the bigger the effect will be.

Make Your Retirement Plan More Efficient

I have built thousands of plans during my career, and I really enjoy designing plans. When I first began working in the field, I worked for a big company focused on investments. They set clients up with a personal advisor, and we'd meet with them ostensibly to design the greatest benefit for their retirement. But in reality, the main goal was for the company to make as much money off clients as they could. Once they'd retire and start pulling money out of those accounts, no one was assessing the effect on their tax returns.

I have learned over time that how you draw on certain accounts can have a big effect on how much money you are able to save. It's like getting the best mileage out of your car. If it's not tuned up, you're not burning fuel efficiently. With just a few tweaks, however, the car runs better, and you don't have to buy as much gas. In the same way, you want to adjust your retirement plan to be as efficient as possible—going further on less fuel.

You don't want to burn through those retirement accounts and nonretirement accounts that you saved during forty years of work. You could end up going from full to empty within ten or fifteen years. You want to know you have enough savings and income to make it through. Examining the tax piece of your plan and adjusting it can make it more efficient. That account will last longer, you'll keep a little bit more in your pocket, and you'll be able to enjoy the lifestyle you envisioned throughout retirement. You've worked so long; you do not want to arrive in retirement and find you can't do what you want because you don't have the money for it.

How Social Security Is Taxed

Because Social Security is taxed at a lower rate potentially than other types of accounts, in some cases, you should draw Social Security earlier to keep your taxes down over time. This is another piece of your retirement plan puzzle, and how it fits with all the others can make a big difference.

Social security is taxed as what is called *provisional income*. We can apply a formula to calculate when and how much to draw, but I won't put you to sleep by explaining it in detail.

They have made it more complicated than it needs to be. I use a few software programs to make planning easier.

The main point for you to know is only a certain amount of your Social Security is taxed. The rate is based on your income. So if you have a little bit lower income, not much of your Social Security is taxed, if any. If you draw a lot more of certain retirement accounts, more of that Social Security is taxed. Sometimes we are able to start Social Security earlier for a client. Many books and magazines on retirement recommend taking Social Security later in life, because you are just paid out more from the system.

If you wait to draw, the incentive is that Social Security's monthly payments to you will be higher. But if you follow that advice, you may be taxed more while drawing from retirement accounts that require you to draw. Sometimes it makes sense, based on your situation, to draw Social Security earlier for the tax benefit and take less from retirement accounts. This is a big piece in the planning—figuring out when to take Social Security based on your situation to give you the best advantage.

Taking Social Security early may not be the right solution for everyone. Everyone's plan is a little different. We always do an evaluation to make sure. For some people, taking Social Security later is better because they might have saved too much in other retirement accounts. Keep in mind it all comes down to lifestyle and how we can plan the draw. You can't really save too much, but depending on the kind of account you hold your savings in, you'll be taxed at a higher rate on that money when you are forced to take it out at age seventy-two, which is the required minimum distribution.

Accounts Are Taxed Differently

Different accounts are taxed differently. This is important to keep in mind when designing your plan with your advisor. We know your lifestyle costs you a certain amount each month, on average. So we need to generate from all your sources a certain amount of income required to maintain your lifestyle.

There are several kinds of accounts that can be incorporated in your plan:

- Social Security
- Pensions
- 401(k)s, IRAs, and the like
- Nonretirement accounts
- Roth accounts

Earlier I mentioned Social Security is taxed using a provisional formula. Your 401(k) and your IRAs are fully taxed. That means if you are in the 22 percent tax bracket, any money you draw from those accounts will be taxed at 22 percent. If you pull even more, that rate increases accordingly. Now, those nonretirement types of accounts are taxed two ways:

1. Growth. If you sell off an investment, you will be taxed anywhere from 0 to 20 percent on the gain—the brackets are 0, 15, and 20. It depends on how much you are drawing.

2. Dividends. These fall on that 0–20 percent tax rate too.

Roth accounts are considered retirement accounts. You pay taxes on those funds when you first contribute, and when you draw from those accounts, you pay no taxes, as long as you have had the money in there more than five years.

I think you'll agree that this is a complex picture; it takes more than one easy calculation to figure out which accounts to draw from. Sometimes a person comes to me and says: *I have already paid taxes on my Roth, so that is where I am going to pull all my money*. But they do not realize it will cause a problem down the road. Drawing from a mix of different accounts and starting Social Security early may save them tax money over time. Most people don't want to work through all the math or know that they can gain an advantage. Our tax code is difficult. That's why our expertise is essential.

Putting It Together: Find the Lowest Tax Rate Over Time

If you do not plan, you could lose control of how much you pay in taxes. We envision calibrating your retirement plan as a math problem. We know you will be taxed a certain percentage in each area. We average the costs and income for each account over time and weigh them all together. We find the right mix for you so you pay the least over time and keep the most in your pocket.

When is it best to draw on the various accounts?

We help you understand when it makes the best financial sense, depending on the specifics of each kind of account. We've already discussed some of the factors in considering when to draw Social Security. We also help you learn when and how much to take from nonretirement accounts and from the Roths. For the 401(k)s and IRAs, there is a Required Minimum Distribution that obliges you to take out money when you reach age seventy-two.

You may feel stuck with elements of your plan set a certain way, meaning you might have had an old investment that restricts how you draw from it. In most cases, we can simply build the other pieces around it. If you have saved too much in those 401(k)s and IRAs, what we call the *Required Minimum Distribution problem or the seventy-two-year-old problem*—in which the IRS forces you to take money out of those accounts at age seventy-two—we want to fix the problem ahead of time. If you forget to take the money out of those accounts, you can get hit with a pretty hefty penalty on top of your taxes. So, we want to mix these elements together for the best outcome. We want to find the lowest tax rate based on mixing the different types of accounts.

Extra Savings: Enjoy, Give to Beneficiaries, or Donate

Now that we have done the planning over a long period, your savings are building. We know by running the strategies outlined above, you're accumulating more money in your accounts. That creates a good problem: you need to figure out what to do with it. Most people will spend some on an extra trip or invest a little more in renovating or maintaining their house.

But when many clients save extra, they give away their money a little bit earlier—to beneficiaries, to their kids, or to their favorite charities. This newer strategy arose in 2019 when the Secure Act was passed. It gave people who had the retirement accounts a little advantage. That's when the age for the Required Minimum Distribution was raised from seventy and a half to seventy-two, creating a little more time before forcing you to take that money out. However, at the same time, they stated your beneficiaries—not including your spouse—now had to take that money out at a faster rate. They must take all the money out within a ten-year period.

That means if you save a million dollars in a 401(k), and you gain tax savings that, by the time you passed away, totaled $1.5 million, your beneficiaries must take all that money within ten years. In most cases, beneficiaries are children in their fifties and sixties, still working and making the most they have made in their career. The Secure Act basically compounds an issue for your beneficiaries: now they have to take all the money you left them out of those accounts quickly.

I feel bad for a client who has worked their whole life to save money and build it up only to have the IRS end up with more of their money. It makes me feel sad. I hear many clients say they want to give to their children earlier and see them enjoy it. Later on, the kids will not receive a big chunk, and they won't be taxed at a higher rate. But not everyone thinks that way. Some people are of the opinion that it's better to amass funds until they pass on. But everyone is different. Just like everyone's plan is a bit different.

About the Author

Ken Tumolo possesses a long-held passion for helping clients attain financial security and independence as they plan for their retirement years, because he has always believed that everyone deserves a secure and independent retirement. Ken is a CERTIFIED FINANCIAL PLANNER™ and holds the Series 66 license, as well as Life, Health, and Long-Term Care licenses. He also has a bachelor's degree in Financial Services and an associate degree in Electrical Engineering.

Ken's talent for paying attention to detail fueled his early career running a small technical business for fifteen years. His main duties there included planning and projection-based budgeting, which was perfect experience for his move to the retirement planning world. He had already learned how to project and budget for the unexpected that sometimes happens in the business world.

Ken likes to help prove to his clients they are going to be okay. He gets satisfaction giving them that peace of mind. Ken feels his clients need a reason for their investments, and they must fit a plan that will get them through. He likes to take the time to build that plan and get to know the clients and their circumstances. He wants them to understand the plan. If he is building a plan they understand, then he knows they can rest assured he's doing right by them, and he is truly acting as a fiduciary, producing for them what is in their best interests.

With Ken's retirement planning methodology, all the pieces fall in place: the estate planning, the tax planning, and the investment portfolio segment. If there is a chance to do something earlier to help potentially save taxes in the future, Ken wants to make sure clients plan for it. If there is a more efficient way to draw accounts to produce tax savings, he wants to execute it. His goal is to provide his clients multiple ideas, advantages they may not be aware of, and various ways to manage their accounts to get them through retirement and possibly pass on assets to family or charities.

Away from the office, Ken is an avid fisherman and enjoys hanging out with his family. His three boys are older now, but father and sons still get together as much as they possibly can. Ken and his wife enjoy hosting family events, and as odd as it might sound, he enjoys doing projects around the house, like building decks and remodeling. Ken also enjoys running—not competitively—but to take in the scenery and relax.

The S.M.A.R.T. Approach: Live, Lead, and Invest for the Best Life Offers

by Vincent Virga

This chapter is premised on the book *Pioneering Portfolio Management* by David Swensen, the chief portfolio manager for the Yale Endowment. Toward the final stages of the financial crisis in 2009, I stumbled upon his book, and it taught me what true *asset class diversification* is. Up until that point, I thought true diversification was represented by the typical pie chart: some stocks, some bonds, some mutual funds, and that's that. But David Swensen opened my eyes to asset classes that went far beyond just stocks, bonds, and mutual funds—essentially, the importance of not having all your eggs in any one basket.

From that point forward, I gathered the strategies for managing investable assets used by institutional investors, university endowments, and pension funds and applied them to a Main Street level, making them accessible to investors like you and me. Still, the basic approach can best be described as not keeping your eggs in any one basket. That is the premise and the foundation on which I designed the S.M.A.R.T. Approach Planning Process.

S.M.A.R.T. stands for:

- Simplicity
- Measurability
- Accountability
- Reasonable Results
- Teamwork

Most people think when I reference the *invest* part of my motto, "Live, Lead, and Invest," I am referring to only the financial aspect. But folded into that concept as well is the ability to invest time and energies and emotions into others. Investment should not be conveyed solely as stock market investment, but it should also include investment in the well-being of others.

Sustainable and Reliable Sources of Income You Can Never Outlive

In this section, we learn what sustainable and reliable sources of income are. Many brokers and advisors build a templated, off-the-shelf stock/bond portfolio of seventy/thirty or sixty/forty. They believe this will provide sustainable and reliable sources of income through a dividend portfolio. I mean no disrespect to advisors who work this way, but unfortunately, this approach is *not* sustainable and reliable. Another investor may rely on multi-unit apartment complexes that collect rent. Well, that rent is here today but may not be tomorrow—not sustainable, not reliable.

The two areas that can be sustainable and reliable are *pensions* and *social security*. We teach our clients to create for themselves their Personal Pension Strategy (PPS), using similar tools that they may have had from a pension with a former employer. We find income or sources of income for clients that neither spouse can never outlive. We help ensure they maintain control if something catastrophic happens to both spouses. If you have a corporate pension, you collect a payment. If you predecease your spouse, your spouse can potentially receive that payment. But if you both leave this earth simultaneously, you lose that pension.

In building a PPS, we can create an income stream for spouse number one. That income can continue for spouse number two, should spouse number one pass away. But more importantly, we can arrange matters so that if something catastrophic happens to both spouses one and two, whatever remaining value of that PPS does not end with them; they actually maintain control over it, even at death. It is a powerful way of taking away the house advantage, so to speak.

Fee, Risk, and Tax-Efficient Investment Planning

Most investors in mutual funds, for example, do not have a clear understanding of what their underlying risks, costs, and fees are. If asked whether they are familiar with what is called a *net expense ratio*, most people have no idea of what it is. Almost 99 percent of folks who come to my live events do not know. It is an annual fee that mutual fund companies charge, in essence, to keep their lights on. This charge is not specified on any statement.

The *turnover ratio* is another potential fee. Most investors have no clue what a turnover ratio is, but it is exactly what it sounds like: It is how often the mutual fund manager turns over that portfolio. There is nothing wrong with turning over; it is part of managing that fund. But most people do not realize every time the manager turns that fund over, there is an inherent cost. If folks own those mutual funds outside of their IRA, not only are they paying costs and fees in turnover ratio, but they may also be incurring potential taxes in capital gains and dividend taxes for the potential gains in those funds.

Most folks are not aware of the impact of fees and taxes for their portfolios. I walk my clients through a risk stress test. It determines their willingness for risk over the next six months. Quite often when we meet folks for the first time, the amount of risk they are willing to take is not in line with the amount of risk they are taking with their current investment portfolio. There is a science behind the risk stress test that I referenced. It is premised on what is called the *Prospect Theory*. The Prospect Theory won the Nobel Prize in Economics in 2002. It takes an objective and nonemotional assessment of one's willingness for risk over the next six months.

Healthcare Planning

As a fiduciary, it is my moral responsibility to ensure that prospective new clients or, quite frankly, anyone who comes through our doors, understand options they have pertaining to Medicare planning and Medicare supplements, as well as long-term care insurance or long-term care insurance alternatives. We walk our clients through a list of resources to audit their current Medicare supplement plan during their enrollment period to make sure it is the most cost-effective and efficient plan for the next year.

Long-term care may be cost prohibitive and may not make sense. There are incredible tools and strategies that provide long-term care benefits as an ancillary part of the underlying investment strategy.

Be sure to discuss healthcare, Medicare, and long-term care options with your fiduciary. It is an important conversation that should not be overlooked.

Income Tax Planning

At any point in time, the president and administration in office have the potential to introduce major income or tax-planning tsunamis that may come to fruition, and we must be cognizant of changes in tax law. We cannot bury our heads in the sand. We have been having this discussion since the beginning of 2020, because we know the Tax Cut and Jobs Act of 2017—a congressional revenue act amending the Internal Revenue code of 1986—is scheduled to end in December of 2025.

We know income tax rates are likely to increase as of January 1, 2026. So we have been conversing with our clients to plan for that tax code to be unsettled and our tax rates, potentially, to go back up to the pre-2017 rate.

The administration at that time will have to create a new plan that will affect taxes right across the board, including:

- Marginal income tax rates
- Step-up basis
- Capital gains
- Estate tax

Many sections of the IRS tax code we have at our disposal can provide the opportunities for federal and state tax-free income flow and, depending on which state you live in, tax-free estate cash flow. Also free? The provisional tax. Cash flow generated from certain strategies will not be going against the taxes you would have to pay on social security benefits. And then also, as of today, they are free of legislative risk.

As well, we are planning with our clients for how income taxes affect their IRA money. With a traditional IRA, they have options. Taxes may incur on typical IRAs over the course of their lifetime.

There are three taxes most people do not consider regarding their IRA money:

1. At age seventy-two, you are required to take your RMD, your *Required Minimum Distribution*. This forces you to take a portion of your retirement and pay tax on it to the government.

2. If you do not need those RMDs to sustain your standard of living, more than likely, you would invest those proceeds into more investments that incur tax number two: potential capital gains and dividend taxes.

3. If you are working with a trusted advisor who has managed your family's financial wealth well, at the end of the rainbow there's a pot of gold you've left for a loved one, and—guess what? They get hit with tax number three: potential inheritance and estate taxes.

The choices you have are to do nothing and pay those potential taxes, or there is what we call the *optional tax*. In some cases, the gap between the two is huge. The government loves 401(k)s, 403(b)s, and traditional IRAs because they will give a little break on the seeds and then wait until you are retired to tax you on the fruits. If you do not pay taxes and you do not take the withdrawals, they penalize you by 50 percent. So it is a great game if you are on the government side of things.

Legacy and Estate Planning

My two parents came here off the boat from Italy over sixty years ago. They both came here with a grammar school education and only a few hundred dollars in their pockets. Over the course of their lives, my dad came to be respected as one of the top contractors and bricklayers here in our community. He was respected for his work ethic, his integrity, his character, his workmanship, and his leadership.

As is true for many people, it wasn't until after my father's early death at age seventy-one that I appreciated and recognized some of his remarkable characteristics and accomplishments. He created the most beautiful buildings, shopping centers, and homes and could read blueprints, all with a simple grammar school education from Italy; he did it just as well as formally trained architects and engineers. My mom never learned to read, never learned to write, never learned to drive, and she raised three of us.

These people were focused primarily on managing and building their family and fulfilling their life dream here in this country. When my wife began working at an insurance agency, we brought a life insurance agent to my parents' house to talk to them. They did not want to have anything to do with it. They refused to have a conversation about it because of an immigrant superstition.

When I got into this business, I tried again to talk with my parents about planning for their future. I had to drag them to an attorney just for a basic will and living will, and to declare who would have power of attorney. Beyond that, they did not want to do any planning. None whatsoever.

I did not grow up with a silver spoon. I usually tell people I grew up with a wooden spoon that was used for two reasons: 1) Sunday sauce, and 2) the back of the head of the middle child—and that was me. My father's legacy was that wooden spoon. He did not leave me a pot of gold or a wonderful estate—he left me over $45,000 a year in additional expenses for me to take care of my mom's needs. That is a direct result of their refusal to plan for the future and for the inevitable. That is what I inherited. I vowed then in both my personal life and my professional life that I would never, ever, allow that to happen to another family ever again for as long as I am on this Earth. With most folks I meet, I start the difficult conversation about their plans.

I ask them simple questions, such as: *Do you have a family or estate plan in place?*

Most folks do not think about their retirement and end-of-life plans because, just like my parents, they are superstitious or procrastinate for some other reason. But, like I always say, you cannot buy homeowner's insurance if the house is burning, and you cannot buy car insurance at the scene of the accident.

I make it a point for any person who comes into my office, any new face I see in my office, to make sure they receive at least a complimentary, no-obligation, one-hour consultation with an estate attorney to make sure their estate plan is in good order. You can dive more deeply into the topic and explore tax planning as part of the estate. The two intertwine. But I never want you or anyone to ever go through what I had to go through.

About the Author

As the President of PFS Wealth Management Group, Vincent Virga is focused on helping his clients work toward their financial and retirement dreams through a well-thought-out strategy for retirement income.

The published author of *The S.M.A.R.T. Approach: A 5 Step Process to Life, Leadership and Investing,* Vincent has also hosted a weekly radio show, "The S.M.A.R.T. Approach to Retirement," on 970 AM, The Answer in New York, and iHeart Radio. He has been seen in local and national media affiliates of ABC, CBS, Fox, and Wall Street Select for his respected industry knowledge.

Vincent has more than thirty years' experience in the financial services industry, growing and developing close relationships with mentors in all areas of financial management, financial planning, tax-reduction planning, and market alternative investment concepts. Having worked with individuals in the area of wealth management and asset protection strategies, Vincent has been better able to serve his clients' needs in a world that demands unconventional approaches to building long-term financial security.

He lectures extensively to other financial advisory professionals about nonconventional approaches to wealth accumulation and preservation, as well as to the general public, through his energetic and entertaining informational workshops. He holds Series 63 and 65 securities licenses and is an Investment Adviser Representative. Vincent is also licensed for insurance and variable products in multiple states including Florida, New Jersey, and New York.

Vincent has served on the Financial Advisor Council of the Financial Services Institute (FSI) in Washington, D.C. FSI advocates for Main Street Americans' access to objective, affordable financial advice, delivered by a growing network of 40,000 independent financial advisor members. The Financial Advisor Council comprises several of FSI's independent financial advisor members from throughout the United States and advises the organization on the impact of legislative and regulatory issues on independent financial advisors and their clients.

Vincent is a lifelong resident of New Jersey who now resides in Naples, Florida. He has been married to his best friend,

Camille, for more than twenty-nine years. They have two children and enjoy spending as much time together as possible.

Advisory services offered through Madison Avenue Securities LLC (MAS), a Registered Investment Advisor; MAS and PFS Wealth Management Group are not affiliated companies. MAS does not provide legal and tax advice. Seek competent legal and tax counsel for your specific needs.

Investing involves risk, including the potential loss of principal. Any references to protection, safety or lifetime income, generally refer to fixed insurance products, never securities or investments.

Insurance guarantees are backed by the financial strength and claims paying abilities of the issuing carrier. This is intended for informational purposes only. It is not intended to be used as the sole basis for financial decisions, nor should it be construed as advice designed to meet the particular needs of an individual's situation.

Our firm is not affiliated with or endorsed by the U.S. Government or any governmental agency.

The Importance of Taking a Total Approach to Managing Your Wealth

by Graham Wickham

Total Wealth Management is a total approach to managing what is important to you, including all aspects of your financial lives, through all the stages of your life.

To better explain this, I like to use this analogy: When you paint your house, you don't only paint one side. You paint all sides of the house. Total Wealth Management is the same way; it's that holistic approach to all stages of your life.

What are the components of Total Wealth Management? There are five elements we consider in Total Wealth Management:

- Investments
- Tax strategies
- Retirement planning
- Estate planning
- Risk management

Let's begin by discussing ***investments***. Investments are the items that we put inside of the accounts to grow, or generate income, to accomplish your needs, goals, and objectives. Investing is about defining what you're trying to accomplish—whether it's growth, income, or growth and income. We also want to consider how we position those investments to achieve our desired result for as long as we need to achieve it. We should consider the allocation and how you diversify your investments.

The next component is ***tax strategies***. While it is your legal obligation to pay taxes, there are strategies to ensure that you do not *overpay* taxes and keep more of what you have worked so hard for. A good general first step is to look at exemptions, deductions, and any credits that you can take advantage of.

Next, consider your employer-sponsored retirement plans, such as a 401(k), 403(b), 457, and SEP or the Simplified Employee Pension plan. Then you could explore opening individual retirement plans that are not through your employer, such as a Roth IRA or a Traditional IRA. With a Roth IRA, you wouldn't get a deduction on the contributions you make to it *today*, but if you meet certain qualifications, it's tax-free for you down the road. With the Traditional IRA, you have the opportunity for deduction, but it will grow tax-deferred and will be taxable upon distribution later.

One thing that is not often communicated to investors is how you should position certain investment assets in certain accounts to minimize your tax liability until you need those assets. For example, ETFs (exchange-traded funds), indexes, and individual stocks are inherently tax efficient; they may be better positioned in your taxable accounts. Mutual funds and taxable bond funds could be positioned in your retirement accounts that are taxed later or never taxed, since they are less tax efficient.

Since we don't know exactly how taxes will affect you or your income down the road, one thing to consider is a *3-bucket tax strategy*: Taxed now, taxed later, and never taxed. In the taxed-now bucket, you could position individual stocks, ETFs, and indexes. The taxed-later bucket could contain your less efficient investments, such as mutual funds, taxable bonds, and the like. And finally, your never-taxed bucket could contain your Roth IRA, municipal bonds, and cash value life insurance.

Retirement planning involves thinking about that next stage of your life. Everyone has a unique vision of retirement.

Without a clear vision of your retirement, how can you plan for it?

We always encourage the individuals we work with and the attendees of our classes that we teach to take a moment to sit back, close their eyes, and actually envision how their retirement looks for them:

- Is retirement an extended vacation?
- Or is it something closer to home?
- When do they plan on retiring?

Those options come at different price points and may need some additional planning to accomplish.

The next steps would be to look at your time horizon, your income needs and your expected expenses:

- What are your income sources to cover your needs in your retirement years?
- How much money is coming in versus your expenses going out?
- Will you need to pull extra income from your savings and the investments you have set aside to supplement your retirement?

So again, it's important when thinking about retirement planning to consider how much income you need, your expenses, your distributions, and the length of time you anticipate needing them. Prior to retiring, it never hurts to do a trial run with a budget to inspect what you expect.

I believe ***estate planning*** is one of the most important topics when considering your wealth management plan. It specifies how you want what you have worked so hard for to be controlled and distributed while you're alive and after you pass.

A good place to start is how you title your accounts:

Are they individually owned or joint owned? For example, if you have an individually owned account, you may want to consider adding TODs (Transfer on Death designations) or PODs (Payable on Death designations). Ensure that your beneficiaries on your insurance policies and retirement accounts are accurate and up to date.

The next step could be adding some additional legal documentation to clarify and customize your wishes. A Will documents your wishes while you're alive and after you pass.

Elements to include in your Will are:

- Advanced directives
- Medical directives
- Guardianship for minor children or heirs with disabilities

Trusts could be added to be even more definitive and restrictive on who receives your assets and how and when they receive them.

The final component that makes up Total Wealth Management is ***risk management***. Remember that *everything* has risks. So, you must define how much risk you're comfortable taking compared to how much you want to pass on to other resources.

When considering risk and investments (stocks and bonds), remember to include various risks, such as:

- Market risk
- Company risk

- Inflation risk
- Liquidity risk
- Opportunity risk

You need to define those risks and make sure you're comfortable with them based on your goals, objectives, and time horizon.

Another risk management mitigation tool is insurance. Insurance is meant to indemnify or make us whole. Whether it's auto, homeowner's, business coverage, life, or health, you want to make sure that each of those policies accurately covers the loss you're trying to mitigate. It's essential to understand how much risk you are willing and capable of absorbing compared with how much you want to pass on.

Why is it important to have a team that takes this Total Wealth Management approach?

The answer is simple: When you work with a team that takes this approach, you're not dealing with a *Jack of all trades and master of none*. You consult experts in each component of Total Wealth Management working with you on all aspects of your financial life.

- The insurance team handles the insurance products to mitigate your risks.

- Your financial team implements and allocates investments into accounts to accomplish your goals and objectives. This may involve additional investment analysis, cash flow analysis, and evaluating your risk tolerance.

- Your legal team makes sure that your wishes while you're alive and after you have passed are granted in the fashion that you want.
- Your accounting team or CPAs assist you in evaluating tax strategies to keep more of what you have worked for.

It's important that each one of these areas of expertise come together collaboratively to accomplish your personal goals and objectives and are managed throughout your life. No questions are left unanswered; no t's are left uncrossed, and no i's are not dotted. While this is not a guarantee that your desired outcome is achieved, this approach could increase your odds of reaching your goals.

The best way I can explain the benefit of having a Total Wealth Management strategy is with this analogy: When planning a big trip, you usually don't start out without having an idea of how you're going to get there. You create your itinerary. You look at your map and determine when you must leave to arrive at your destination on time. You determine at what points you plan to take breaks and stretch your legs, fill up with gas, and so on. As you would plan your vacation or holiday, you plan your wealth. While wealth is not always defined by the dollar amount, you want to plan what's important to you every step along the way, so you know where you're at, where you're going, and where you're going to end up. A Total Wealth Management approach helps to get you there while keeping you in the driver's seat.

About the Author

For more than forty years, the Wickham Financial & Insurance Services companies have been a part of the Marietta Business Community, serving the financial needs of thousands of individuals, families, and business owners in the Cobb County and greater Atlanta, Georgia, area.

Forged by his parents before him, President and CEO Graham S. Wickham continues the proud tradition of serving others through the use of affordable insurance products and has expanded the family of companies to include financial planning products and strategies to address broader financial needs.

The Wickham Family's abiding approach to business and life is demonstrated in the following business philosophy: seek to understand, then to be understood.

As an investment advisor representative and insurance agent, Graham is dedicated to helping his clients achieve their personal goals and objectives. Graham and his team listen to their clients. He says, "We first have to truly understand what matters to them, so we can work toward creating comprehensive plans that focus on their financial goals. We take a total approach to our services and focus on helping our clients solve financial challenges, not on pushing products."

Graham and his skilled team of insurance and financial professionals work hard to develop trust and focus on helping clients understand that their goals are obtainable. Many clients feel that in order to achieve goals, there is this complicated web of strategies. He and his team help break things down into their simplest form, explaining complex financial matters in an easy-to-understand way.

Graham earned a bachelor's degree in economics from Western Carolina University. An accomplished speaker, Graham regularly presents public literacy workshops on retirement planning, investment planning, and risk management strategies. Notably, *Atlanta Magazine* has recognized Graham as a "Top Five-Star Wealth Manager" every year since 2009. Graham is a member of the Kiwanis Club of Marietta and the Cobb County Chamber of Commerce, where he participates in the CEO Round Table and is a Partner in Education.

Graham and his wife live with their son in Smyrna, where Graham spends as much of his free time as possible outdoors. He enjoys kayaking, biking, paddleboarding, running, hiking, camping, and adventure racing.

Wickham Financial Group, Inc. is a Registered Investment Adviser.

The commentary in this publication reflects the personal opinions, viewpoints, and analyses of the Our Firm employees providing such comments and should not be regarded as a description of advisory services provided by Our Firm or performance returns of any Our Firm's Investment clients. The views reflected in the commentary are subject to change at any time without notice. Nothing in this publication constitutes investment advice, performance data or any recommendation that any particular security, portfolio of securities, transaction or investment strategy is suitable for any specific person. Any mention of a particular security and related performance data is not a recommendation to buy or sell that security. Our Firm manages its clients' accounts using a variety of investment techniques and strategies, which are not necessarily discussed in the commentary. Investments in securities involve the risk of loss. Past performance is no guarantee of future results. No advice may be rendered by Our Firm unless a client service agreement is in place.

Preparing for the Ticking Tax Time Bomb

by Jude H. Wilson

When most people talk about financial planning, they typically focus on investments. At least, that has been my experience. Getting the highest possible return seems to be the topic most investors are interested in. It is my firm belief that too many dollars are being lost unknowingly and unnecessarily.

This is called *opportunity cost*. When we meet with clients, we want to achieve the best possible return and we want to capture all the dollars that are leaving them. Dollars that could be used to increase their returns—hard-earned dollars that are already there. Without knowing all the strategies available to them, many are paying too much in taxes.

I want to share with you how to:

1. Capture those opportunities.
2. Plan for the likelihood that taxes will probably increase dramatically in our lifetime.

It is every American's responsibility to pay their fair share in taxes. They should pay no more than their fair share and learn to use every available tax strategy to reduce their taxable liability. There is a difference between *tax evasion* and *tax avoidance*. Tax evasion is illegal. Tax avoidance is our right to reduce taxes to the lowest legal limit.

The Ticking Tax Time Bomb?

Our federal income tax system began in 1913. Believe it or not, the highest tax bracket in 1913 was only 7 percent. The highest tax bracket historically has been a staggering 94 percent. Today, we are at the lowest tax environment we have seen in over a generation. But the danger is that taxes may increase as the deficit increases. The more the government spends without having a strategy for reducing the deficit, the more likely federal taxes will rise dramatically. That's why I call it the *Ticking Tax Time Bomb*. Much in the same way Paul Revere is credited with alarming everyone: T*he British are coming! The British are coming!* I am yelling, *"Higher taxes are coming! Higher taxes are coming!"*

I hope to help everyone who will listen prepare before the Ticking Tax Time Bomb explodes on their retirement. The current United States deficit is the highest our country has ever seen. Our country's comptroller is like the accountant for the U.S. government. David Walker was a U.S. comptroller during both republican and democratic administrations. He has said there is a high potential that tax rates could double in his lifetime. Now, he could be wrong, but he said there is a four-letter word that describes why tax rates could double in his lifetime. What is that four letter word? *Math.*

Pre-Tax, Post-Tax, Tax-Advantaged . . . Where Are You?

Everyone should understand how to create tax diversification. The first concept to understand is the *order of money*. Money flows, as far as taxes are concerned, through three tax funnels:

1. **Pre-tax Money**: Money that enters the pretax funnel is not taxed by the federal government when it enters this funnel, and it is not taxed while in the funnel. However, when the money is withdrawn it is taxed at current ordinary income tax rates. Examples of the pre-tax funnels are 401(k)s, IRAs, and 403(b)s—typical retirement accounts.

2. **Post-tax Money**: The post-tax funnel is sometimes called the *investor funnel*. Money comes in post-tax, meaning you have already paid tax on those dollars. The growth on these funds can be taxed while in the filter and when withdrawing. The base amount invested is not taxed. If you have received dividends, or if you sold that investment at a profit, you will be taxed on those dollars. Most often investor dollars are taxed at less than income tax rates. Examples of post-tax accounts are (nonretirement) brokerage accounts, bank accounts, and real estate.

3. **Tax-advantaged Money**: For money that goes in the post-tax funnel, taxes have already been paid on these funds. Both while in the funnel and when withdrawn, those dollars are not taxed. The government sets limits on the amounts and strategies for assets put into this funnel.

We have heard of investment diversification, but rarely do people talk about tax diversification. If you are like most people, having a strategy for placing assets in each funnel can protect you from the Ticking Tax Time Bomb.

Protect Your Nest Egg From Higher Taxes

Now that you understand the order of money, it is easier to understand what you can do to protect your nest egg from higher taxes. Tax diversification, through making use of the three different funnels, is the place to begin. Next, understand where your money is housed.

Is the majority of your money in the pre-tax, post-tax, or tax-advantaged funnel?

The Roth IRA and 401(k) are two of the biggest advantages we have available to us. Most people do not understand the differences between the Roth 401(k), and IRA. They sound similar, but they are actually cousins of each other. The Roth 401(k) allows people to contribute regardless of income limit. The Roth IRA has caps for contributions based on income levels. The Roth is an account that falls in the tax-advantaged funnel. It allows people to put money in post-tax. While it sits in this account, there are no taxes on the growth of the money. The money that is withdrawn will never be taxable, not to you, nor to your heirs who may inherit the account.

We highly recommend creating tax diversification. You may wonder whether you can contribute to a Roth because you have a large IRA or 401(k). *Roth conversions* are a potential solution to moving money from the first funnel that will always be taxed—regardless of how high tax rates rise in the future—to the third funnel, the tax-advantaged funnel, where our money will never be taxed again. However, you need to understand the process to take full advantage of this opportunity. In addition to Roth, there are several other possibilities, too many to discuss in this one chapter.

One possibility is a Health Savings Account (HSA). Most people utilize the Health Savings Account to pay healthcare bills. Another strategy is to use your HSA as a holding place to use later for tax-free income. Deposit money into your HSA and pay your healthcare bills out of pocket, while saving receipts for all your health care bills. Instead of reimbursing yourself from the HSA immediately, wait to pull the money out. That is one way to accumulate tax-free dollars for the future.

Taxes Are On Sale!

It is painful to pay tax bills, but believe it or not, today's tax rates are some of the lowest in over a generation. The highest tax bracket in our country's history was 94 percent. The highest current federal tax bracket is only 37 percent. This is attributed to the Tax Cuts and Jobs Act (TCJA) of 2017, which will expire December 31, 2025.

There are three possible outcomes when it expires:

1. Congress and the president vote the TCJA into law, and these tax rates remain the same.
2. Congress and the president come up with an entirely new system to replace the Tax Cuts and Jobs Act.
3. Congress and the president cannot agree to anything, and the Tax Act expires.

At the end of 2025, TCJA will automatically expire, and tax rates will revert to what they were prior to 2017. Regardless of what our politicians choose, it is inevitable that tax rates will increase from where we see them today because of the deficit. In other words, taxes you pay today are **On Sale**.

The Tax Management Journey (Seven Steps to Understanding and Managing Your Taxes)

We implement a proprietary process called the *Tax Management Journey*. It is a seven-step tax strategy map that represents opportunities to review strategies for reducing your taxable liability, both currently and to reduce the effect of rising tax rates in the future.

The seven steps on the *Tax Management Journey* are:

1. **Understanding the Order of Money**. The order of money is what we discussed previously: how money flows into three different tax funnels.

2. **Measuring Your Tax Bracket**. Most people do not understand how the tax brackets actually work. It's highly important to understand the bracket system to take advantage of the lowest possible tax rates.

3. **Avoiding Marginal Tax Traps**. A small increase in income can cause a drastic increase in taxation.

4. **Allocating Tax Sensitive Assets**. Determine how to invest assets with a tax-wise focus.

5. **Gifting Strategies**. Use opportunities to convey wealth while avoiding excessive taxation.

6. **Paying Taxes Now vs. Paying Later**. The choice is yours.

7. **Managing Dynamic Tax Brackets**. Maximize the use of your marginal tax brackets. We use this map to assess how to reduce your current tax liability or prepare to reduce your liability in the future. Every step on the journey is important to creating tax diversification and reduction, as well as protecting your nest egg from potentially high taxes in the future.

About the Author

Jude Wilson, CWS®, BPC™, MBA, is Chief Wealth Strategist at Centrus Financial Strategies. He has more than twenty-four years of retirement planning experience. He earned his bachelor's degrees in marketing and finance from Florida State University, an MBA from the Rollins College Crummer School of Business, and he holds his Series 7, 63, and 65 licenses. He is also a Certified Wealth Strategist, CWS®; a Registered Representative with JW Cole; and is Bucket Plan Certified with Clarity 2 Prosperity.

Securities offered through JW Cole Financial, Inc. (JWC) Member FINRA/SIPC. Advisory Services offered through JW Cole Advisors (JWCA). Centrus Financial Strategies and JWC/JWCA are not affiliated entities. Centrus Financial Strategies and JWC/JWCA are not tax or legal advisors, and this information should not be considered tax or legal advice. Consult with a tax and/or legal advisor for such issues.

Conclusion

Most Americans don't have access to independent sources of information to help them plan for and live their best retirement.

We specifically selected the advisors in this book based on their unique skills and industry expertise. No matter where you are in your retirement journey, you can utilize the sound advice offered by the authors of this book to help you make your retirement whatever you want it to be.

The advisors who authored these chapters offer insights that can translate directly into a piece of your retirement strategy.

Most pre-retirees and retirees don't know where to begin. They are not really sure how to make good course corrections or even what questions to ask their current advisors.

Our hope is that you have made notes and highlighted, or flagged, ideas that pertain to you as you read this book.

Follow up with the person who gave you this book because they demonstrated a desire to educate the public by taking time, energy, money, and resources to share the information you need to retire well.

If nothing else, we hope that each person who reads this book takes some sort of action to improve their retirement strategy. Unfortunately, many people who are given the independent information they need to make smart investment decisions choose to take no further action. We challenge you today to use what you've taken from this book to better your circumstances, as well as those of your family and your legacy.

About the Editor

Mark Edward Gaffney is the Founder of MEG, a boutique marketing, coaching, and consulting firm for the financial services industry. Mark's Elite Advisor Client List reads like a Who's Who of financial advisory firms. Since 2002, he has coached, consulted, and trained thousands of financial professionals across the United States. His image and brand advertising agency approach to financial marketing has made him a prominent authority throughout the national advisor community.

With more than twenty-five years' experience in marketing, Mark's list of credits includes: renowned national marketing strategist, executive producer of numerous television shows and radio programs across the United States, keynote speaker, and co-author of the best-seller, *The Winning Way*.

Mark has worked with multi-billion-dollar corporations as well as startups and financial business entrepreneurs at all phases of development. His marketing strategies have generated billions in production for his financial clients.

Made in USA - North Chelmsford, MA
1308981_9781945446863
03.21.2022 1541